KORRA IS LIVE

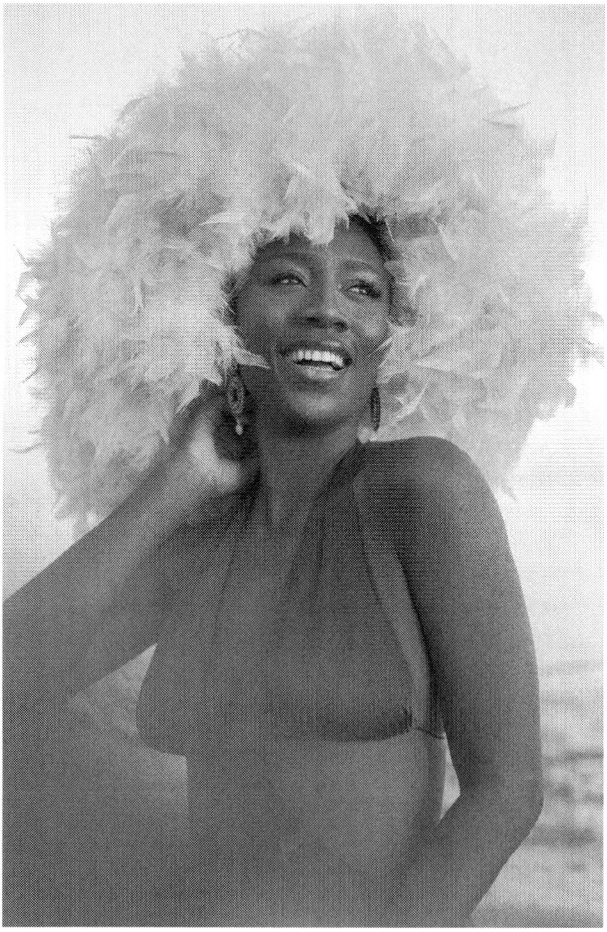

The Inception

I am probably going to look back at this book and ask myself 'Why did you do this Chukwufumnaya'?

I most likely will be vilified for the rest of my life for coming out with my truth. I'll probably lose half my fanbase and be canceled.

Truth is, it took an incredulous journey to get here, to heal, I have to adequately release. I write

this for my daughters to read and learn from my mistakes. My choices and how I navigated through them, I write this for my future self to see I did it.

For the sole purpose of not getting sued, some of

the names in this book will be changed.

One of my earliest memories from childhood was crying and looking at the other kids through my window. I wanted to play with them so bad. That

never happened. I was never allowed to play with the other kids. Not until my mom died. Yup, that happened. We had a house help, Aunty Gloria. She made my hair and made me feel loved. I was the third girl child, I have 2 elder sisters and a little brother. I always felt very invisible. Aunty Gloria always had a way of making me feel seen. One Day, she bought me a lollipop when I was sick with malaria. This is equivalent to having the flu.

This was the only time I had ever been allowed to have one, it was one of those types that had bubble gum in the middle. It was so amazing. It tasted like freedom. Aunty Gloria and my mom had some sort of altercation, she had burnt the beans on the stove because she wanted to go make her hair. Aunty Gloria had come of age, she was ready to be her own 'Madam'. Soon, I didn't see her anymore. She was gone. My mom had granted

her her freedom which I believe at that time was a couple of sewing machines and some money. I secretly blamed my mum. I still miss Aunty Gloria to this day.

I grew up in a government residential area, reserved for the elite accountants in government-registered banks where my father held a very high position. We were comfortable.

My parents cared a lot about education and they made sure that they

invested that in their kids, I spoke French and had a

German tutor before I was 11 years old. My mother always knew what she wanted for her children.

I went to Military school. Nigerian Army Officers Wives Nursery School, Command Children's School, Command Day Secondary School. I am an Ex- Commando. Discipline was the order of the day in those schools. I remember all students in our class

being told to lie down under the sun as the soldiers flog several strokes of the cane made from the branch of a guava tree.

This tree branch had a characteristic to grab onto your skin as soon as it landed on you. The pain from this whip was level

100 yet I remember being flogged daily for every and anything. This was and still is considered normal where

I'm from, I don't like this about us. Soldiers laying all the kids down and flogging us with 3 mouthed whips for being too noisy was a daily occurrence. This made me normalize trauma, and equate love and nurture with abuse, genuine care with brash words and physical torture.

I grew up in the strictest most religious household you could ever imagine. To put it in context, my father was a devout Deeper life

Bible Church member. In that church, disciples weren't allowed to watch television, own nice things, or even use deodorant. All these were considered things of the World. For the longest time, we had one computer. That CPU quickly became my very good friend. My father knew I had a thing for computers so he made sure I always had one. He paid for computer lessons and insisted I learned some programming. I wanted to know more. I

wanted to see more. Your only source of information that was allowed was the 'outline' that was circulated from the headquarters of the church, bi-weekly. The members were the most judgmental, hateful humans I have ever witnessed in my life. I was brutally raped by one of them. More on this if you stick with me. Most of the kids I grew up with in that church turned out to be the sickest, most demented adults ever. You will

understand my plight as this book progresses.

My mother was the local rebel. She had her hair permed in a congregation that perceived her to be

Delilah herself. She had I and my sisters in colorful high heels before we were 10 years old. We stood out, my mom made sure of it. Now that I am older, I see my mum was silently protesting this church that didn't even allow my mother pierce her daughter's ears

till she died. It was intense. It still is. Church still exists. Crazy. I know.

Just a little inside scoop on what growing up looked like. My mother took mothering to another level, she lived for her kids and we all knew this. I have 2 sisters and a brother. I am the last girl.

We never ate out, snacks or anything were prepared from scratch by my mother.

My mother cultured our yogurt from scratch!

She was a Nurse, and a Business Woman and demanded nothing short of perfection from us. If I came home with 2nd position in school, I was sure to answer for it. We were all amazing scholars until hell broke loose and my mother died. Cancer was the diagnosis. After a long battle with the disease, she gave up.

Growing up, it was inexplicable, we all knew what was required of every one of us. My siblings and I knew we were only allowed to be nothing short of greatness. It was an unspoken rule. I remember almost peeing my pants when I didn't come first position in school and I had to take my report card back home to my mum. I thought I was going to get a whopping. I didn't.

My mother was a disciplinarian, to say the least.

I was 8 when I found out I was a princess. The Obi, my grandfather had just died and all his children from all his wives were required to come back to the village for his burial. We traveled for what seemed like years in my little mind to this super tropical village right in the heart of the Delta. All I remember from that trip was a very huge lemon my mother sliced open one hot afternoon, we sat under this tree and my mother explained how she had never seen the fruit grow anywhere else in the world, I remember thinking to myself, ' this the biggest citrus fruit I have ever. I met a lot of Obidi and what was surprising was the sheer amount of cousins, nieces, and relatives I had that I didn't know existed. The burial was short and we went back to our home in the city.

My mom died quite early in my life. All I remember was my dad crying. His loud cries plague my dreams. I had never seen him cry till the day she was laid in state. He cried like a baby. His cries filled up the entire village. I don't remember crying. I was angry, I was so angry because it was a long and draining battle against cancer, and still nothing. It drained us, financially, emotionally, and physically. Most especially my dad. At one point my father came home with 'snake oil', this was from a python one of the Fulani men has caught.

My father went to the ends of the earth trying to fight the disease. After my mom had completed one round of Chemo. We put the snake oil on her tumors after a bath. To date, I have no idea how my father bought that. He heard snake oil could help, so he found it. He bought it. His wife had to have it. It was an extremely difficult time, to say the least. My family gave everything, yet, my mom still died.

My mum would go in and out of remission,

oscillating between great health and days of weakness and being bedridden, one beautiful day, I stopped by my favorite flower bush, and on my way back from school, plucked some flowers for my mother's beautiful long hair. When I got home, she was so strong and dancing. She had made us lunch like the old times and I was so grateful. We danced to Destiny's child, and I

couldn't contain my joy, I put flowers in her hair and it was a good day. The very next day, it got so bad, she couldn't get out of bed.

She said something that haunts me to date. "Fumnaya, I know you will be happy if I died, you will be free".

Now that I am older, I understand that she was dealing with symptoms I had no idea about, but as a child, I was so tormented by those words. Yes, I love to

play, I have always had this bubbly persona. I don't need you to die to do that mommy. I was angry, angry at myself, angry at the world, angry at my mom. How could she leave us? Time passed, time healed, and we moved on.

Chapter 2

Trauma Kid
Where It all started.

I had a lesson teacher, Uncle Francis. Uncle Francis was my common entrance Tutor, he was supposed to be my guide to make sure that I passed all the examinations that I needed to ace to go to secondary school in Nigeria. Uncle Francis taught me from the UGO C UGO, if I was doing well I got praise, if I was doing badly, I got a spanking on my hand. We used to have lessons at my dining table,

One fateful day, towards the end of our time together, Uncle Francis told me to stand up, I thought he was going to reprimand me for a question I had missed, I was afraid, I got up, he got up too, this was weird, Uncle Francis was weird, we all knew this, but this time something was different. He came close to me, very uncomfortably close to me, and told me to hold on to my dining chair, so I did. He inched behind me and started to thrust, he

started slowly and then proceeded to briskly dry hump me so roughly. Then he stopped, I turned and saw a puddle form on his trousers, he moved away, instructed me to seat down, leaned in, and whispered

' tell anybody and I'll kill you. He left.

He continued to do this for a few months, dry-humping me after every lesson. I wasn't too young to know what was going on but I was too afraid to tell

anyone of my very strict and holy parents, or my

very unique, quick-to-report-for- favor sisters. I didn't want them to be disappointed in me, and I also didn't want to be killed by Uncle Francis, so I stayed mute. The exam came, I passed, and Uncle Francis stopped coming over. I erased it from my memory. Erasing was easier to do than talking. I was 10 years old.

Lesson learned at that age, is if I endured long

enough and kept quiet through anything, It will eventually pass. In therapy, ii found that this is the most toxic lesson a child can learn, and learning to stand up for your truth while giving room for expression is all I can truly pass on to my daughters.

With my mom's death came a radical shift, in my life. We started to do poorly in school as our mother who was the disciplinary figure of the family had

passed on. I was determined to keep doing well. it broke my dad's heart to see us not excelling as much. I couldn't stand the grief on his face. I began to try hard at school on my own. I answered all the questions in class, but this rubbed off badly on some of the girls in my class who couldn't stand me getting all the attention of the teachers, they threatened to beat me up if I kept on answering the questions, I didn't stop, in my mind, it was their happiness over my Dad's happiness, there was no comparison. So they trailed me all the way home, cussing and yelling horrible insults behind me, I didn't dare look back at them. I caught a glimpse of one of them, she was my next-door neighbor, Turayo. She was the leader of the pack. They insulted every part of my body, from my head to my feet till I got home, It was a 45-minute walk from hell. This accounted for the top 3

most traumatic childhood experiences. Bullies go around leaving eternal psychological scars they do not know.

With my mothers death came freedom. Freedom like never before.

Freedom like never experienced. With that freedom came new siblings. My father got married again. He needed some free babysitting for his 3 hot girls and stud son who had become the talk of the estate as the new reigning,

free-to-hang-out, next in line to be ravished by the testosterone-driven boys in the neighborhood.

My father got married to his elder brother's wife who was deceased. I am from a royal family, in the OBIDI FAMILY, It is customary that when a brother dies and he has a brother alive who also has a deceased wife, it is 'ok' to have both families joined in holy matrimony. My mother had just died, but it was a necessary alliance as we were 3 young girls who were at vulnerable ages and we needed a mother's guidance. My cousins became my step-siblings. Weird, I know. It wasn't long after the families merged that I began to feel the shift in the family dynamic. The new mother was good to us, she was very religious and had 2 sons who lived with us at the time. To the best of my knowledge, I think she loved my father, however, resented the love my

fathers so shamelessly proclaimed for his kids. You see, on my mother's deathbed, she had instructed my dad to take care of their kids, my dad had done just that and sometimes took it overboard. As a 19-year-old, I sometimes woke up to the sound of my dad in my bedroom killing mosquitoes that tried to feast on me at night, my dad's love was palpable. The new mother was a Nigerian Pastor and leader of an all women's

fellowship, slowly but surely she started to complain that all my father ever talked about was what he was going to do for his children. 'My children, my children, my children' she would complain as she made fun of his love and obsession with the wellbeing of his children.

This became a staple argument in the household. Every morning and night, it was one fight or the other.

My father is a very meek, yet stern classic African parent who grew up in the palace, in the village but moved from the village to a catholic school, obeying his mother's bidding. He was the only son of the Obi's last wife. The love child. Youngest of his brothers. His mother wanted a different life for him. He became a chartered accountant and soon after married the love of his life, my mother.

In a story he carefully curated for my sister and I, he met my mother as an Immaculate gift from God, she was a virgin, and God's precious gift to him for life. This made me and my sisters laugh as we knew he was just trying to manipulate us into not trying sex until marriage but that story stuck with me throughout my teens.

I had a lot of friends after my mother died, we changed schools, changed

homes, and moved in with my stepmother who had graciously allowed my father to take over her bills and livelihood as soon as they tied the knot. We the kids did all the chores in the home, beauticians, estheticians, and cleaners. We became hired help in the name of home training. I starred in several movies at the time, Surulere was the heart of Nollywood and my step-brother was a budding filmmaker. My father on the other hand just wanted some free babysitting for his girls while he worked all day at the bank to afford his new lifestyle.

We lived on Nnobi street, Surulere, Lagos.

We lived with a new family.

And this is where the story begins.

A lot of our integration into this family and the details that ensued between the cousins turned brothers and my elder sisters are not

my story to tell, I will leave that to the appropriate custodians of the gist and concentrate on my own story, I believe I was 13 years old at the time. I had just started my period and I was given the welcome to womanhood meat. A tradition in the family where, once you get your period, you don't get 'the talk', you get the biggest piece of meat for dinner.

I will not go into full detail about what happened in

this time frame as some stories are not mine to tell. Some of the most traumatizing experiences of my life happened during this period.

Let us begin with the arrival of a distant cousin, let's call him ED. ED was easily the most charismatic young adult I had ever met. He wrote poetry and was a comic too. He was amazing to me, he stayed with us for a while, and then it happened. My sister caught him fondling my tits in the middle of the night. I was fast asleep thank God.

We ignored it and did nothing about it. We moved on. Life went on.

This one time, it was Valentine's day, Nancy being the most popular girl in secondary school had valentines gifts from everyone and their father in the school. We had so much chocolate it was insane. I was the designated chocolate eater, we had to finish it before we

got home because our cousins turned brothers were very vicious with accepting anything from any male, valentines day or not. I ate so much my tummy started to ache, we hid the rest under the stairs, when we got home, our cousins turned brothers who were told to babysit us by our father stripped us naked and flogged the living crap out of us. I was 14 and Nancy was 15. Now in therapy, I realize that, that singular humiliation meted

to us by Men put in charge to protect us, was one of the reasons I ever got into an abusive marriage in the first place. I equated love with humiliation and safety with torture. The formative years of any child 12-20 are very important for the psychological well-being of the child. Be careful what you subject your offspring to In the name of home training.

My dad's new wife had an opinion about what time I

had to be home. After weeks of verbally inciting my father to discipline me as I was getting 'spoilt' under her roof, one day I had an ushering job that took longer than I thought it would. I made sure to tell my dad, 'Going to be a little late dad' I texted, but no reply. That's weird. He always replied. I showed up at home at about 10:30. As I walked into the house, I had a punch on my stomach that sent me straight to the floor. My father had hit me,

he proceeded to kick me several times on the floor, I felt like a robber that had just been caught stealing. I had to run for cover, what had gotten over him? He had never touched me before. He accused me of the worst things, prostitution amongst other things. I couldn't believe he had no trust in me, I thought he knew me better than that. I resolved that I could never fully trust him after that. I left the house for Unilag as soon as I could

manage and I never came back, in retrospect, I think he was manipulated by his wife. He is still the best dad ever though, just not superman like we all want our fathers to be, just human like you and me with our flaws.

My journey began at the University of Lagos. I wanted to be in the Arts. My dream faculty was the Creative Arts but I was so afraid to admit this to my father. You see, where I am from, being a Musician or dancer isn't a thing of repute. People assume you cannot have a good life with the meager salaries of an Artist, with a few exceptions of big artists who struck fame, being an upcoming artist is likened to the fate of a beggar. All an African parent sees are those Rastafarians at the beach singing with a guitar for tips. My father wanted me to be entertained and not be the clown. My first-hand encounters with musicians

were dancing to the tune of the Musicians who would come to our tent whenever we visited the beach to sing to us for some tips and donations. I knew my father wanted more for me. He wanted me to study Law or something more 'white collar' and more related to a professional course.

After having an amazing course score in JAMB, an exam you needed to score high in to be admitted into any University, I chose the University of Lagos. I had heard many cool stories and was sure that this was the school for me. I very quickly got the shocker of my life on how tribalistic and unfair the intake process was as there were a limited amount of spots and so many students to tend to.

I eventually got an admission into the University of Lagos but it took my father pulling some serious strings as I was not in the 'cashment' area.

Cashment area is another name for tribalism, I wanted to go to a school that was in the west, I was from the Delta, I was not of the Yoruba Tribe and so I was not granted admission because my Jamb score didn't meet the cutoff for non 'cashment' states, Tribalism is huge in

Nigeria, it is one of the factors responsible for the dilapidated nature of some sectors in Nigeria. One could be the most competent for a job but that

job will be given to a less competent person just because of tribe afiliation. Favoritism based solely off of tribe is a norm.

Admission into the University symbolized FREEDOM, coming from a Military Secondary school and graduating, as 'Best Arts Student', I thought University would be a breeze. It wasn't. In my first semester, I finished with a 0.64 CGPA. This was equivalent to graduating with a 3rd class. I was immediately jolted back to reality after seeing that result. I was shocked. I made a deal with God. I told him if I never copied off anyone, and never cheated in any of the exams, he would have to give me a 1st class or at least second- class upper. We made this pact and we signed it in prayer. And so began my deal making relationship with my creator. True to the deal, I graduated with honors.

Let's call him Big G.

Big G and I had an understanding, he gave me the talent, vision, drive, and intelligence, and in return, I didn't do any funny business to get to the top or compromise my value system. I agreed.

Chapter 3. UNIVERSITY GIST

In UNILAG, I was that churchy, ever-so-bubbly girl who was friends with everyone. I was in the school fellowship and was super serious about joining the dance group at the time. I remember passing through all the ridiculous hurdles to becoming a dancer in my fellowship, only to get to the one-on-one interview and was asked directly by some overzealous church enthusiast if I was a virgin. I was so surprised.

From a tender age, my father always gawked about how he married my mother as a virgin, he always expressed how this made him a very happy man. He didn't know but I silently swore to be a virgin when I got married. I wanted my husband whoever it was to gush about my virginity long after I am gone, as my father did my mother's, at the slightest opportunity he got.

I intended to save my virginity as a priced gift for my husband on our wedding day, LIKE, HEY... surprise! My body is brand new and untouched by your sexual pleasures. In retrospect, thinking about saving my body, not for me but for a man, makes my belly churn a little bit, however, let's not digress.

The interviewer asked me again, ARE YOU A VIRGIN?

At this point, I was in my second year at the

university. I was a virgin. I didn't know much, but I

knew that question didn't seat so well with me, I felt violated. In front of this panel of people. I walked away and never looked back.

I had started to notice attention from the opposite gender become stronger as I got into living in the school hostels, soon I was receiving a lot of gifts from prospective boyfriends. One of them that stood out the

most was Dami, he had gone to the school cafeteria and figured out my favorite place to eat, he then went ahead and paid for a month's supply of free food for me. I thought that was beyond thoughtful, so I gave him a chance. Dami was my first kiss. It happened at the waterfront in Unilag.

Let's just say, Dami was not the one. We weren't in the same faculty so we just kind of drifted apart. This was something I had no control over and I

was fine with it. He had a lot of friends, and when we broke up they will always tell me to go back to him. He had been sending his friends to apologize on his behalf and I thought that was weird. Today, I don't even remember why we broke up. All I remember is I had to do a lot of cleaning up of my reputation after him. Lesson learned, never let a man pay for your bare necessities. The delusion of ownership sips in quickly.

I moved on quickly and soon after I met another charming heart stealer whose name started with D as well. He seemed to be everything that I wanted but I knew in my heart of hearts that I could not give D what he wanted. We were in the heat of our sexual explorations. Everyone I knew was exploring their bodies, except me. I made a pact with myself to stay a virgin till marriage. I was determined to keep this promise to myself, I wanted

my husband-to-be to sing my praises to the 7 seas, to my kids, and to everyone just like my father did my mum. I was so in love with D and he was in love with me too. We spent hours talking on the phone with each other, we deprived ourselves of sleep, just to listen to each other breathe. There was a snag, I knew I couldn't give him what he wanted, whatever a guy his age wanted. I couldn't have sex or be sexually active, he was a very sensual man, I

knew it was only a matter of time till we wants to go

all the way. I decided to graciously exit the relationship, I left D to keep my promise to myself and my daddy, Virgin till I Get married was the goal. Signed and sealed contract with me to God's ears.

I had a very close friend in the school of nursing, at the time, for this book, we will call her V, she and I were very close, we attended the same church and I visited her regularly at her school, she was so cool in my opinion. One of my favorite friends at the time. I shared all my secrets with her, she knew about my pact with myself. I was very proud of my decision to stay a virgin till I got married. It was no secret, I was very proud of my decision and I was too naive about what sharing it with a girl who probably was not a virgin might

trigger, V was sexually active. She had a boyfriend at the time and they seemed to be really into each other. One day V hits me up. She says her big brother S will be in town and that he wanted to take us all out to dinner. I was excited. A 19-year-old who had just started dating and exploring restaurants outside of school, this was so thrilling. The week V announced her brother's arrival in school, a young boy got shot in the

Shodeinde hostel in Unilag. V's brother S was a cultist and notorious yahoo boy. A yahoo boy is a cyber scammer, A cultist is a word used to refer to people who belonged to different deadly fraternities. I was scared and thrilled by this 6 feet + male who had so much power and commanded so much respect amongst his peers. He was so rich as well, pilling up to the front of my residence with one of the sleekest cars I had ever been in.

He came by and grabbed us all, whisking us to this restaurant. At this restaurant, we ate some Chinese food and had a great time. I was so happy. This was my first official date, it was at a fancy restaurant, I had my best friend at the time with me. We had so much fun. I still have a photo from that night somewhere on my social media. You're going to have to scroll back to a very long time ago and guess the

social media. Everything was going great on this date, S seemed to be the focal point as everyone did whatever he said, on the table were V, S, and some other guy. Everything was good until

I started to feel very dizzy. At that time, I was very light-brained and didn't drink a lot. I remember ordering one Nigerian Chapman for the night, it was very strange that I could bearly get up from my seat, I tried to get

up and got so dizzy I had to seat right back.

V came to me to help me up a flight of stairs, then

all of a sudden I was in a room with just S, V was nowhere to be found. It was at this point that my eyes cleared. I knew something was wrong, I reached for the doorknob and S violently knocked me down, I started to scream V's name, but she never showed up. It was at this point it dawned on me what was about to

go down, straight I went on my knee and started to beg, and S laughed.
' What are you begging for' he said, "just lay down AND LET US GET THIS OVER WITH" he yelled.

I started screaming for help.

No one answered, and I continued to scream. "Anybody please!" at this point I was profusely crying and yelling. S inched towards me and laughed, he grabbed his phone,

placed a call, and put it on speakerphone. "E get one girl for here wey no wan corporate, he casually said", the voice on the phone blurted back, "Baba where you dey, we dey com".

At this point, I knew I had only 2 choices. if I didn't lay there and get raped by just S, I was going to be raped by S and a battalion of cultists, I resolved my fate and calculated my next move. "Please please, don't

tell them where we are, I'll be quiet" I begged shamelessly.

S told the boys to simmer down, I proceeded to lay on the queen-sized bed that was in the center of the room. As I inched towards the bed, I heard a loud hit on my head, I was in shock. I had already accepted to be raped by this man but he had just hit me on my head so hard that I slumped onto the bed, he yanked me violently and then started to

rip my clothes off, he tossed me around like a rag doll. I was numb, the taste in my mouth was a mix of blood and anguish, the tears began to flow and I couldn't stop it. Right then, all the promises I made to myself and my dad were being violently broken by a man I barely knew for a plate of Chinese fried rice. The betrayer V who had carted me over to her heinous sibling was nowhere to be found.

He pounced on me, his giant frame hovering over me, he reached down to my panties and ripped them off, then with the speed of a bullet, he tore into me with his "surprisingly small for his frame" fully erect penis, causing me to bleed all over the bed, I let out a cry of pain, which he proceeded to cover with his huge arm, I had to wiggle off from underneath his arm to catch a deep breath. He was going to choke me. With about 7 strokes, He was

done in 2 minutes, and with a loud thud landed on my side and was out like a light, snoring up a thunderstorm. I looked over at his penis and my hymen casually sitting on it, staring right back at me on his cap. He was gone, and for a brief moment, I thought of ending him, with the bedside lamp, right on his huge head.

I got up, it was 4 am, I picked up my torn

undies, and my phone and left the

room, walked outside, and saw the cleaning staff right there. The Chinese restaurant was located in a hotel where they had been lodging. I had no idea in my mind I wanted to ask, why? Why didn't you help me? Why didn't you call the authorities? But instead, in shame, I snuck out.

Hard- wired in me was the fact that if I was molested, it was my fault. As a dis- virgin, my value had dropped. Who was I to question anyone? The entire

thing was planned by my so-called best friend V who I so carelessly bragged to about my virginity. It was a 10- minute walk away from the University of Lagos gate. This walk is etched in my memory, I couldn't stop crying, my bruised privates brushing against my torn panties as I felt my entire worth crumble to the ground.

As I approached the school gate which traditionally opens at 6 am, I

was trembling. It was 4:10 and I thought I will

have to stand there till 6 am, however, the security guard on duty took one look at my face and opened the gate immediately. I walked in without a word, straight to the school's health center where I told the nurse I had been deflowered, a pamphlet, morning-after pills, and a few sachets of paracetamol later and I was back in my room. As I approached my room entrance, there was V,

begging, "I'm so sorry". I asked her, "where did you go"? There was no response.

Then came S in his fancy car and a trunk full of groceries, had his sister bring the bags into my room, all these made me laugh. I was so confused why he was gifting me all these hours after he violently raped me while his sister listened in from her room. He begged for my audience which I granted,

he said he wanted to know if I am angry, and that he thought his sister was lying when she told him I was a virgin. I just sat and listened in silence. He bought me a blackberry phone days after and was asking to be my Boyfriend. My rapist becoming my boyfriend was sick but a part of me was wondering "Well, since he has already taken the best part of me, according to what my society dictated, he might as well take it all. In this twisted unfortunate turn of events, it never occurred to me to tell anyone, let alone go public with it. I could never.

I would have been viewed as damaged goods, probably never get married, and be vilified and judged by every soul as the girl who got raped. After weeks of gifts from S and incessant apologies from V, I decided to never tell anyone, I shaved my head, cut the ties, and became a new person. Started to

learn self-defense, got serious with my dancing, got vicious with my music, and never looked back.

S kept trying to be my boyfriend, this was weird. I entertained the idea for a little bit, in my mind, my father had wanted me to be married to the taker of my virginity, in my case it just happened to be a serial rapist-murderer who was very fetish. I know this because he came to me one day after whatever he

did for his job and told me that his priest (fortune teller) had told him I was going to be very famous. I shrugged, to be honest, I was numb, I couldn't stomach nursing a relationship with this man, and my time with this man was a blur, I think my brain has erased this.

In my quest to never be that vulnerable again, I found Capoeira, I was named Korra, the one who could do all. In my

Joda. Everyone called me Korra,

and it stuck. Korra Was Born, Chukwufumnaya could seat back for Korra to take over, and Korra Did.

When I was young I watched Shakira's music video for 'Whenever Wherever', I was so obsessed. I always have been in love with Shakira, but something about that song changed the entire fabric of my being.

I was determined to be a Dancer and Singer just as good or better than Shakira. My first quest was to find someone to teach me how to dance, after Nancy bought my first dance shoes from the UK. All I wanted to do was to learn old, exotic styles. One day I was walking around the school's sports center when I saw a man dancing, some styles you don't see every day. He was doing some Ballroom Samba, I had never seen a type like that in real life, I was so fascinated, for the sake of

this book, let's call him Jack. Jack was a big fish in a small pond, a peacock- like character who always had to show off. He and I dated for a while, but I soon realized I was in a relationship with myself. He was sleeping with all our students, as we taught salsa together. I began to learn dance with him and we opened up a company together where I was the accountant. I was not getting any payments and I assumed that this was

because I was part owner of the company as I was there from its inception but I was an employee without pay. I kept on working for the passion of working and dancing but it soon dawned on me that I couldn't continue. One night after a long night of salsa dancing, he got physical with me, he wanted me to take a bath and I didn't want to, so he yanked me so hard on my shoulder, and to date, I still nurse that injury. One day Jack invited me over to see

his parents, we wherein his dad's room, and everything was peachy, having conversations, Jack and his mother stepped out briefly and Jack's father casually let his hands slide across my breasts. In shock, I laughed it off and proceeded to weasel my way out of the room. That was the beginning of the end between I and Jack. I never told him what had happened.

As you already recognize, when I leave, I never look back. Recently I learned from therapy that it is the fight or flight response. I packed my bags and never went back to that studio.

Chapter 4.
SHADY OPPORTUNITIES

I met an older man. Let's call him Mr. O, when I say Mr. O was old, I mean old. He was 85 years old with the heart of a little boy. Mr. O just loved to look at me, he wanted to stare at me all

day, so I made him pay my performance fee which at the time was N150,000 per day, I would go over to his house filled with an armed security detail and dance and sing to him. He was so happy when I danced. He told me to make sure to never dance for free. Mr. O was amazing until when he started to be creepy. I got a call from one of his staff telling me to show up at the airport. I showed up, passport in hand, and next,

you know I was on a first-class flight to Dubai.

I began to travel with Mr. O, I always insisted on my room even though I knew I could end Mr. O with a simple Gallopante if I felt threatened.

Things were great and I was a happy travel companion with no strings attached to my naivety, but as you know, nothing goes for nothing. One day in Lusaka, an armed security detail comes over to my

room and knocks hard, It's 11 pm, and I use the

peephole, 'who is there?' I blurt out, the chief wants to see you in his room, he returns. I smile to myself, I knew this day was coming. I am coming, I replied, then proceeded to double lock the door and tuck myself in nice and tight.

This sent Mr. O a clear message he didn't quite like.

We came back to Lagos on a flight back and he

made sure I flew economy to get his disappointment across. I was just happy to have toured as much as I did with Mr O.

I was not getting booked for performances as word on the street was I didn't put out, I was a cock tease, that never went all the way. I was getting broke. I decided to attempt to begin to travel alone. No security or first-class ticket. My first stop was Dubai, I shopped for gigs and auditioned,

wasn't long before I started to dance. I belly danced at the Marina with a bunch of beautiful women from various countries, it was indeed an honor, my music began to take off and before I knew it, I was performing at the Burj Al Arab, then for the Sultan in Muscat, then back to Dubai for some more belly dancing, I was getting famous.

Mr. O shows up in Dubai and leaves me with the

biggest tip I ever did receive, he then proceeded to fly me to

Oman a small city in the middle east, where I met the most powerful men I have ever met to date. I Performed my music. All this made me very grateful to Mr. O. It wouldn't hurt to bring down some of my walls. I decided to go spend the night with Mr. O. To date, I don't know why I did that. Mr O, had a saying, every human has a price, just make them an offer they cannot refuse. In

retrospect, I guess it was just the first time a man had given so much to my craft without forcefully trying to take anything back.

I'm in Mr. O's penthouse suite enjoying all the room service I can stuff in my mouth when Mr. O asks that I lick his butthole. All the color left my face and lips. In his defense, he said he didn't want sex and was too old for it but this was all the wanted. I was not only shocked but flabbergasted.

All my senses were tingling. This has to be some fetish buhaha, my ancestors were singing and screaming hell Nah.

At this point I already had, my own residence and gracefully asked to freshen up and proceeded to sneakily exit the premises.

Turns out it wasn't a fetish at all and he just wanted a princess to lick his ass literally. I had no idea he knew who my grandfather was and since they probably were the same age, he felt the discrimination towards the royal family in the village, he, on the other hand, was a merchant who rose to wealth through the work his hands, I respected that about him, but he wanted to pay for bloodline royalty to lick his Ike (aka Nyash).

So that happened. We move.

Deciding to do music in Nigeria as a young woman means you are now the national cake and everyone

wants a piece. Promises to make me a star in exchange for sexual favors were a regular Tuesday morning for me at the time. This one time,

I went to a notable radio station somewhere in Lekki phase one to promote my new release. The MD at the time shamelessly sends over a room number to a hotel nearby. This was so effortless to him, I think he was a pro. So many promises of fortune and fame in exchange for some sex, with every bid to promote my music, there was a roadblock of some sort, the trade-off was usually money or sex. I was not offering either so I peaked at the point sheer talent could take me in Lagos. The rest was man- know-man.

Chapter 5 TRAVEL BUG

In Dubai, I had to undergo some racism but my

technique had always been to ignore and it was working just fine. I was etching every day toward my dreams, and I was loving it. The only snag was, I was not making as much money. It was hard for me to continue with the lifestyle of the rich and famous without actually being rich and famous. With only a Bachelor's degree to my name, my family chimed in and ordered me to go do my masters in Shanghai.

My university was in a not-so-popping province in Zhenjiang, not a lot of people spoke English and I was so lonely, the culture shock was real. It was really hard to learn applied economics from non- English speakers. There were no churches anywhere and the ones I found were just designed for photo ops. I went in there one day and prayed for a husband. That night I swiped right on Mr. J on tinder. The only place I could find English speakers.

My friends all wanted to be in Shanghai, Mr. J had a nice loft in Shanghai. We were young, wild, and free. We partied a lot,

Shanghai had one of the best nightlife scenes in the world. There was a club called M1nt with live sharks in the walls.

I dropped out of my master's program and started to move from place to place dancing with Mr. J and documenting it. The love was incredible. I had never felt anything like it. I was in complete awe of this man and I couldn't believe how someone could show that much love. We couldn't be separated. It was incredible. We drank a little too much and sexed like rabbits but that was not a concern because we were enjoying every second of our lives together. He asked me to move in with him 2 weeks after meeting him. This was when the red flags popped but I was too in love to care or notice.

One night we had gone out partying. He complained about how I stared at black men a lot when I was with him, in my mind, I was thinking, I see a black man or woman once a month in Shanghai as we were a rare find, pardon me if I stare a little longer than I should at my kind.

As we walked out, a Nubian man in all his glory, tried to talk to me disregarding the man with me, that was a little rude of

him. I gracefully reminded him I had a man, squeezed Mr. J's hand for reassurance and we walked out of the club. As soon as we got out, he called me a BITCH, left me in the front of the club, and started running into the night. I was in utter shock. No one in my life had ever called me that, at least not to my face. I had to navigate Yangping Lu at 2 am without any cash, through the help of a good samaritan, thankful for the survival Mandarin I had

learned. He had my phone in his pocket and everything. I eventually found my way to his apartment and saw him outside fuming and cussing. He was pacing back and forth, red as a tomato, and saying gibberish. I was so freaking shocked. I proceeded to pack my things. I had just moved in with him and canceled my lease, I didn't know what to do. He begged. Blamed it on my drink being roofied. I had never seen anything

like this. I soon got to learn it was a panic attack, according to him.

We would go through cycles of 2 weeks in which he would have these attacks, they would involve a lot of screaming yelling, phone smashing, and fear. I was determined to fix him. I believed that I could. I was not in any way attracted to anyone but him but he had his doubts and insecurities, I soon altogether stopped looking at black people to

keep him comfortable. I did everything I could to

avoid the rage. Yes, That happened.

Mr. J came to Nigeria, killed the animals, met the elders, and married me traditionally. I am Obidi who is of royal lineage, it was simple, he paid my bride price which was $20 or N20 if he was Nigerian because our people do not subscribe to the extortion of the groom or selling of the bride.

It took me 6 months to get to America, Trump had just been elected and Trump's America was on lockdown, in those months, we communicated via video calls and texts. Mr. J, insisted I call him every night before bed, I did this religiously. One night I had gone out and had a wild time, I forgot to call him, and he got so furious on the phone, he turned tomato red again and this time, called me a CUNT. This scared the living Jesus out of me. The last time, he blamed his verbal abuse on me being roofied at the party, but this time; he was completely sober… I think.

I knew I couldn't be married to a man that verbally abuses me at the slightest provocation. My self- esteem will be mush in 1 year of being with a person like that.

This man had already MET MY ELDERS, what do I do?

This time I threatened him, 'if you call me that again, the wedding is off!', I said. It worked! He stopped fuming, piped down, and apologized! I was fighting for a change and I believe I found a solution! We apologized to each other and continued our wait.

That night I couldn't sleep. Every part of my being felt like I made a mistake with this man. He had become more controlling by the day, the persistent name-calling wasn't something I was used to, I grew up with my community very loving towards me. This was alien to me, I was so scared and upset at the same time. The American government was taking its sweet time and I was getting impatient. Something about knowing you are about to leave home for life just brings out the 'I don't give a rat's a**' in you. I was done, but at the same time, I was ready to explore everything I will

be missing. I started to go out more often, I had just recently gone viral and the FAME, which I believe is the most intoxicating drug had gotten in my head. I was out with celebrities, spent nights in private beach houses, and just enjoyed my life every single day of the weeks I knew my days in Lagos were numbered. In retrospect, this must have been very insensitive to my fresh husband who had just moved to a new city, Los Angeles to begin a new life

with me, I shouldn't have documented the life of the party as he struggled, to be honest, I underestimated how hard it was to move to a new city in America, I was young and naive.

One night out in Lagos, it was 5 am and Mr. J had demanded that I call every night before bed, this night though I didn't I got carried away by the champagne rain and my music blaring in the speakers, I got home and crashed. The next

night, a girlfriend of mine invited me out to dinner. I went there and it turned out to be a fancy late-night boat cruise with some of the most influential men in the country at the time. I was both shocked and surprised at such a spontaneous opportunity gifted by the universe, I met Jack.

UNFAITHFUL

Jack was so charming, very hospitable by nature and generous. As soon as he met us, he immediately bought a drink for the table. He was charismatic too. Jack made my night at the party. He was a gentleman and dropped me home. The next day, I got a performance gig. A high- end prestigious gig, one of those, 'didn't haggle your price' gigs.

I was very grateful because a girl just spent so much on her

traditional wedding she had to split 50//50 with her Oyinbo bae in the spirit of equality of the sexes. Turns out it was Jack's private party, I was shocked. I did my job and performed to everyone's heart delight. I was grateful, a shortcut to my heart is appreciating my craft and he did just that.

The next week jack invited me for dinner, and that was the best sushi I had ever had. I had lived in China but it was by far better than anything I had in China. He proceeded to show me parts of my city I had never seen, and I was blown away. It was one of those nights you only see in movies heavily curated to the 'T' by this new stranger. Jack was working overtime and hitting the mark every time.

I had another gig. This time, a stadium gig. One

where I couldn't go myself, I casually mentioned it in a conversation we were

having, next thing I knew, Jack booked an appointment for my hair and nails, I show up and get the most amazing installation and nails I have ever had, at exactly 6 pm, my armed escort and driver pick me up, take me to my gig and then make an amazing video of my performance, I am flabbergasted at how proactive this man is. I am grateful but at the back of my mind, I am thinking, Chukwufumnaya are you mad? What are you doing

encouraging all the advances when your HUSBAND is in America waiting for your Black Nyash? So I pulled the brakes on everything and thanked kind Jack for their generosity and proceeded to wait for Donald trump.

He shows up at my house which at the time, I lived rent-free with my Best friend Rich. Rich was my maid of honor. Rich was also friends with my HUSBAND.

I rush down the stairs and out the door, quick enough to make sure no one saw me. 'What are you doing here'? I blurted. Ignoring the fanciest car I had ever had come visit me. 'You blocked me', he said.

'I didn't realize I did, I am extra sometimes, let's go'.

We drive away, and I proceed to explain my situation. That was when he opened up about being married. Oh my God. That was heavy. We were both MARRIED! Mine was official, no court or white wedding but traditional. We talked for a long time. All the vulnerability spewing left and right. One thing led to another. We cheated.

Right after, I felt like the water that sits inside concrete gutters in Lagos. I felt putrid. Sick to my stomach with myself, I blocked Jack again and proceeded to attempt to erase my memory of my atrocity.

I realized this panic affair must have been an indicator that maybe the love was not right, Maybe if it was so easily tainted, then I needed to wait. Maybe I was moving too fast. I moved in with this man 2 weeks after I met him. It was an internal battle daily. Should I go? Should I stay? Stay where? Here? There was nothing for me here.

4 months later, my Visa got approved. I parked my bags and headed over to

my new life. I am in the arms of my USA bobo living the Hollywood dream, and Lagos is behind me. I am having the time of my life. Everything seems to be perfect. Every night is a movie. We got married in court within 3 months. We were doing amazing. In a bid to impress his Nigerian pop star wife,

Mr. J bit more than he could chew.

Reality began to set in. In less than 6 months, we were homeless. We lived

with a roommate and shared rent. One faithful day, this roommate decided LA wasn't what he wanted anymore and absconded, things began to spiral when we had to pay rent of over $3200 on our own, I had just moved and still earning in Naira. Most of my revenue came from dancing to artists' songs as I was not around my city to be booked for anything. Things took a turn when we couldn't anymore. I, currently number 4 with my

song 'park well' in Nigeria, and my Dr. Husband were homeless in Los Angeles. We started Airbnb. It involved moving around living for weeks at a time in strangers' houses. As beautiful as this may sound, it is no way to live. It took a toll on my mental health but not our sexual health because we were still sexing like deranged rabbits. One morning after sleeping on Mr. Jay's massage table, my entire back cramping, I proceeded

to go use the office bathroom that had become my bathroom as well, Mr jay came in with me, smelled my pee, and said, You are Pregnant. I was shocked. The initial plan was to stay in LA for 5 years before we considered expanding our family, but with my fertile African nyash, all the withdrawal in the world couldn't stop the breeding. I had so many emotions marinating in me. We came to Los Angeles for our dreams, I was currently in

talks with some big record labels and this happens. We decided to keep it but we were homeless and had nothing for our incoming kid. Hustle mode activated. I was just 2 months pregnant and hadn't started showing. I was determined to make life meaningful for my daughter. I met up with an old Nigerian friend of mine, I begged and asked for help and how I could make some good money for hospital bills, and she said

' you no go fit do this kain

work'. At this point, as long as it was earning, and legal, I was willing to do it. It was Halloween and I was a cat- woman for Halloween. Somehow we still found a way to party. The costume was still seating in my box, she told me to get it and she stitched it tight for me, very form-fitting, got some cat woman accessories, and introduced me to the way of the streets.

She soon abandoned me one-week post hustle as

she found out I was not street-wise at all. We would go to the Hollywood walk of fame, strike poses with strangers for tips and donations, she dumped me because she said I was slowing her down and the other cat woman who was her friend had complained about her replacement. I was out in the cold on the streets. The amount of rejection I experienced doing this is enough to knock the sanest human off the wagon. One time I was

taking a picture with a Mexican man who took the liberty of grabbing my right butt cheek with his full palm, he squeezed so firmly, I have never felt so disgusted, I was not allowed to have any altercation with the patrons of the boulevard so I respectfully walked away. I needed a clique. I soon found a team. I rolled with green lantern and batman, they were twins, always fighting and such fun to be around, they took care of their cat. Spider-man who was a Russian crackhead often caught soliciting drugs instead of getting new patrons to take pictures was also in the group. We were a winning team. I would leave the street daily with $100-$150.

CHAPTER 4
WORKING GIRL

After work each day, Mr. Jay will come to pick me up, count my earnings and

add to our savings for June's birth. When I could no longer work as it was impossible to suck in my pregnancy pouch, I saved about $3000, we only needed a few thousand more to pay for June's birth. We paid off the Dr $4800, only to discover that we had to pay another $5000 to the hospital for the labor room rental, this was when I broke. I was at my wit's end with the USA. I had never suffered this much in my entire life. It was

embarrassing to call my family to admit defeat after the entire marriage was already cutting against the grain. We somehow pulled it together ad my time sleeping on my friend's couch was the happiest I had ever been with Mr jay. June came and we started to pull things together, got a studio apartment in We-Ho, and life was great. I was cooking, cleaning, and doing everything a new mom should. Things were looking up with Mr. Jay's business.

One unassuming afternoon, I and Mr. J are having a conversation and we start to go back and forth, the details at the moment are blurry but Mr. J grabs my phone from my hand and smashes it on the wall. My phone shatters into tiny bits. I had no iCloud backup, all my memories of home were gone. He started to pace back and forth, fuming, red and

cursing. It was astonishing and scary to witness, after my phone was broken, in disbelief, I started to weep, shoot, I was right about the red flag I caught, I did nothing and now look at me, holding on to the phone's broken bits. He kept pacing so I went over to help him, my heart pounding at a million miles an hour, showered him, and then learned he was having a panic attack.

I educated myself about the phenomenon and I started to seek ways to help him. I forgot about myself, and the way my heart skipped when he did that. I immediately focused on him. This was what he enjoyed. I teased him about loving the attention as a middle child, but it became worse. My waking breath had to be focused on him. Soon this became a bi- weekly occurrence in the home. I was pregnant and he would slap me, smash, my phone and buy a new one the very next day, my heart would skip and this one time I screamed so loud, the cops were called to the apartment 2 times, each time, he threatened all sorts If I said anything. This particular time, there was an altercation and he was screaming and yelling at me for hours like he always did, I had made a video for an artist as this was my only source of income, and he didn't like a part of the video. After he had called me a whore and cunt for hours, he proceeded to smash my phone right next to June's head. This was when I realized I was not dealing with a sane human. It didn't matter if June's head was right there, it didn't matter if I was pregnant, once he got in that mood, he had to hurt me and nothing was stopping him.

They say hurt people hurt people and someone like

me was very naive about my well-being. I thought I could take the hurt as long as it made my husband feel better, life was hard and I as a wife was supposed to make life better for the owner of my head, this was engrained in my genetic makeup as an African woman, but the physical and emotional abuse started to take a toll on me.

In the heart of Covid, we had been fighting back to back, I was so tired. At this

point, when he was screaming at me, subconsciously, I was trained to make sure I was looking at him. He smashed my phones so many times, I didn't want all of my work and content gone. If I hadn't backed up, It was lost.

I didn't deny Mr. Jay my body, I gave him on demand even when I was not in the mood. This was how I was taught.

We had just moved into a new place with June. It was

barely a week since moving in and he was already screaming at me, I vividly remember begging him to not introduce us to the neighbors like this, but he didn't stop. I tried all the tactics I had learned, at this point I still thought it was an anxiety disorder and he had me convinced that I was the trigger, and before me, he never screamed at anyone, I was the cause and at fault. So I proceeded to try to help him calm down, and he left the house. We had just

moved in, and June and I didn't have a bed to sleep in as we weren't able to move the bed ourselves and he was ok with just sleeping on the floor, after about what seemed like three days of hell sleeping on the floor with my 1-year-old, I went to the other apartment and I picked up the mattress, put it on my car and put it on the floor so my daughter didn't fall sick. I felt so alone that day.

I couldn't shake this feeling of loneliness as I hugged June tight. 'I got you' I whispered in her ear. I started to question everything, myself, my life, and my choices. I had become a housewife that cooked and did laundry. All the dreams that had brought me to this city were completely shattered as he always reminded me of how I was no longer a spring chicken. I was old, I could never be Wizkid, only kids made it big in music, I was too old to matter, how my body was not the same after June and even how saggy my tits were. I breastfed June for a year by choice and I was very happy too but he shattered my self-confidence by constantly pointing at anything I was doing badly.

He had me convinced that I was no longer smart and that my brain was rotting from constantly being on social media. At the time, I was not making

much from my music and dancing, partly because I couldn't perform anywhere as I had a newborn and was at home. My only outlet was Instagram. It kept that flicker of my dream still burning. It wasn't a complete 50/50 but I paid my bills and kept living expenses for us three below $600 a month by being consistent with eating in, I made the healthiest meals in that budget and filmed it in Korra's kitchen, a show I created and edited the

videos with music in it to make sure that my music didn't die, I didn't want to be the statistic, get married and forget your dream. He didn't come home till midnight as usual. And left home at 6 am. I was married but single with a newborn, a cage I couldn't get out of. One beautiful day, while going through my DMs, I saw a message from S, remember S? He violently took my virginity, yes, that S, it read, 'you looked so good in your last video, I feel like raping you again'. I froze, then blocked the account, which shocked my entire nervous system.

When he convinced me that, if I quit social media, I could double our family's income, I decided to quit cold turkey. I went cold, no Instagram, Twitter, or Facebook. Around the same time, I had stopped breastfeeding, as he told me I had horrible saggy tits, I was a mental mush,

spiraling out of control with no sense of 'self' left.

CHAPTER 5

I LOST IT

On day 3 of no social media, no husband, no family, and no connection to anything. I lost it. I had a mental breakdown. In what seemed like 48 hours of hell, I was talking about everyone who had ever hurt me, I was spilling every

single thought I had ever repressed and I was spiraling, one of the most horrific things that happened in this colossal mental mess was Mr. Jay came home and saw me in that state but he didn't notice for 2 days. That was the state of the marriage. Online bliss but shambles in real life. For 2 days, I was mentally gone and he came in at midnight, got up at 6 am, and didn't notice.

I was going in and out of consciousness and when I came back, the first thing I did was try to give June some food because I knew if I wasn't there for her, there was no one else. After 2 days of pacing back and forth the house all day, slipping in and out of my senses long enough to give my daughter a diaper change and some bread, Mr. Jay comes home at midnight, saw that I was talking gibberish, and started to question me, he

asked me any and everything and in that state, I had no control, I spilled everything. The story of my affair came flying out. I had an affair before I came to America. He went wild, all this time, June was on her Ipad. He turned red again and although I was gone mentally, I still remember the fear in me, he goes downstairs and starts to take out my boxes, tossing all my things out.

Get out of my house, bitch.

I ran down, sanity temporarily back, long enough to beg. Please I beg you. Please don't do this. Mr jay pulls out his phone and started to film me, 'Hey Cunt, I am going live now Bitch, how about you tell your millions of followers how much of a whore you are. I was gone. In the middle of my mental breakdown, Mr jay forcefully had sex with me and proceeded to feed me with edible marijuana. I am now realizing that was rape. I

was not sane and didn't give my consent.

I went haywire after the edibles. He claimed he thought that would help me sleep. It didn't.

After all, the taunting had happened at night and in the morning I was quite ready to leave that house by all means. I jumped out the door calling everyone for help. I screamed I am in a cage! I am in a cage! This man is torturing me. I want out! I remember a dog was

walking past and I stopped the owner and

asked the dog for help. I had lost it. The dog looked at me and then looked at Me, Jay. I had completely lost it! An ambulance came and in a couple of minutes, I was out and headed to the emergency room. Bound on a stretcher, repeating different words and singing at the top of my voice, repeating my producer's name, Kayozo nonstop. This is all I remember. Just before the double doors

were shut, Mr. Jay says, ' I love you'. I remember that, but I couldn't understand how love could be this Toxic.

I had lost my mind trying to hold on to this love, the person I was holding on to raped me (again), and taunted me when I lost it.

I had lost my mind betraying me.

Throughout my time in the emergency room, I kept singing and singing. I made

Royal Lamba, in the emergency room. I was chanting the chorus nonstop, alongside my favorite producer's name Kayozo, I couldn't stop chanting. South African rhythms, and war cries from my village, it was almost like I was struggling to stay afloat, stay happy, hyping myself to happiness.

It was crazy literally and metaphorically. It was the peak of covid. Sadly, America was going crazy.

The ER was packed. From the emergency

room, I was carted to the looney bin.

I was taken on a 51-50 hold, it's a place they store the societal delinquents to determine if they will be reinstated with the normal people or locked up in the ward for a longer time. Fuck, I muttered. I am screwed, Nigerian signing dancing princess in a 51-50 hold. On the first day there, one of the inmates sliced a huge portion of my hair and

stuck it to his hair twisting ferociously as he stared deep into my eyes. I looked back at him in utter dismay and fear. F*ck! I am in a deep soup. Otu ti zeh. How did I end up here? Blurry boundaries? Stress? Breastfeeding? Tf?

I was given a journal to document all that had landed me there, I looked back at that journal and all it said was
'Wass' 'Wass'. 'You have to beg Mr. Jay', you have to beg'. Boy was I

completely brainwashed. Now that I think about it. I put my entire life and future in the hands of a sick man who enjoyed torturing me to feel alive. I was released 2 days later, diagnosis after a psych evaluation was a 'THC overdose' from the edibles Mr. Jay had given that night. I was shocked.

Mr jay said I was crazy. If he said so, it must be true. I thought I was crazy. I acted crazy to his delight. We had a lengthy conversation where he disclosed that a lot of American entertainers were crazy, it was very normal to be crazy. He promised he will take care of me. He hid my hospital report from me. I only recently called the hospital for many reports just to have them in case no one believed me.

He narrated how the psychologist had

personally pulled him aside and told him I was Bipolar. I was a little taken aback because

the psychologist at the 51-50 hold told me I just had a mental break and it was completely normal. Mr jay said that he had the best psychologists in the country and the other day when he took me to a party with his psychologist friends, one looked at me and they all concluded that I was bipolar and that I needed to be medicated. This broke me. I couldn't believe how people I cooked for thought I was crazy after just one conversation with me. In

retrospect, boy was I so foolish and gullible.

I never saw the reports from the 51-50 hold, he

said it was a home consultation and he talked to the woman who told him I was bipolar. So I believed him. I must be crazy, why would my husband lie to me?

I was discharged and told to go home. On arriving home, I was told by Mr. Jay that Child services we parked outside and they could take June if I left the house, so I stayed home for 2 weeks with the blinds shut so the DSCF didn't take my kid. I was constantly threatened with them taking June from me. This sort of thing could take me straight back to the looney bin but I consoled myself with frequent calls to family, distracting myself from the cage I had found myself in.

I was invited to a party by a family friend. I gave ample

notice of the invite. I wanted to go, Mr jay said he wanted to accompany me, it was our first night out since finding out about the affair, my visit to the looney bin had delayed talks on the subject and we had just casually brushed over the matter like he didn't just find that out. I knew he was still upset, at the back of my mind, I knew I was under punishment in the house for 2 weeks but I didn't want to let that sip into the perfectly crafted fake happiness I

curated on both my IG feed and in my reality. I wanted to continue faking that I was completely happy living the American dream with my IG husband who secretly enjoyed making me cry as my daughter watched.

We got to the party. It was packed. We started to drink and have fun, I noticed a look in Mr. Jay's eyes, he was up to something. We got drunk, and all I wanted was to make him happy, beg him,

and pacify his anger. Mr jay started to make a scene. Yes bitch, he started to yell, hey guys. Line up and so this bitch can suck your dicks, she's good at that you know, they call her the headmaster. You can run a train on her, she's a whore. Hey guys! Guys! My friends were flabbergasted, I started to make excuses for him, 'he had a little too much to drink please; as I urged him out of the party. On our way out, I was trying to calm him down, but he decked me so hard in the full glare of everyone. I was in the bushes with scratches all over my body. One of the guys charged at him. I immediately shoved myself out of the bush and started to plead! 'Please leave him alone, it's okay, he's just drunk'.

'How is this okay Korra'? My friend replied.

I pulled on Mr Jay, got an Uber and we got out of there before the real men beat him to pulp.

When we got home, I took photos of my injuries and sent them to my sister. He immediately

took my phone and deleted everything. He proceeded to try to convince me about how I had hallucinated the entire night, he said it didn't happen. We had yo call a friend from the last night to confirm that I was not imagining things.

He gaslit my entire existence. 'You did that bro' my friend said. He then apologized, but not as sincerely as he did in the past… This time, it had a hint of, 'get used to this now' undertones in the apology. This is your new normal Korra.

I was heartbroken, it was apparent I was in a very

toxic situation but my entire brand, persona, and even career were tied to this man who was hurting me. That night I hesitated, I pondered on telling my family what I

was going through, the Obidis are not as forgiving as I am and my Husband made a lot of mistakes. I thought long and hard, I looked into June's eyes and I knew what I had to do. I sent the photos of my injuries as I had a deep scar on my thigh to my family group and all hell broke loose. My father, who is a softie, cried, he kept asking, 'Chukwufumnaya, Idi okay'? I replied, I am daddy, but deep down I knew I was in hell. Mr. Jay was still in the

apology phase of our toxic cycle. Right after a

hot abuse session, he was the nicest man on the planet. I could ask for anything and this time, it wasn't a MacBook or new car, or a new home. This time, I wanted out, not just out, I wanted to go home, this American Dream was so horrible, I wanted to go back to my "shit-hole" country because my "shit- hole"

wasn't so shit hole
anymore after this.

This one time, after a
fight. I put on a hoodie
and I decided on a walk,
to clear my head.

On the beautiful streets of
Los Angeles and on that
one walk, I was offered

drugs. A guy who worked at a restaurant asked if I wanted to exchange fellatio for food. I was tailed by the cops until I took off hoodie and they realized I was female. It dawned on me that I was no longer in my neck of the woods, where we had a lot of

problems, but the color of our skin wasn't one.

Leaving home I felt our society was so toxic and I couldn't deal, the crab in the bucket mentality was real and thriving I was happy to be out, but here, I was so sick to my stomach that once I was to be signed to a huge record label, and they got me in the studio to sing, the only thing that came out of my soul was 'Toxic Love'.

I was sick. Tired and Sick.

I got a ticket home and I cried for hours at the feet of my father, It was uncontrollable, my father had to ask me if I wanted to go back, he counseled me that love and marriage were not easy but they brought out the best versions of us.

I needed some fresh perspective so I went to

my friend's house to stay, I told her everything, how Mr. Jay

is trying to pin a diagnosis on me, I thought I could trust her. This friend was so dear to me and had helped at a time I needed so much help. We lived together celebrating the festivities, everything seemed peachy. This was legibly my best friend at the time. All of a sudden she switched on me, it was like clockwork. She started to act so wickedly, I was in her living room speaking to staff, and she told me to get out of her house, in front of my

staff. I was flabbergasted. As I tried to make last-minute hotel reservations for my baby and me, she came and relayed that she changed her mind, I could stay in a guest room I had to share with 4 other strangers. Half the things in my suitcase disappeared. It went from loving friend to downright bitchy towards me, in a matter of hours. I couldn't place where the attitude was coming from and I just weathered the storm until I had to leave, 'you know how much you will be paying if you had to pay for a hotel so you better act right' she said. It was like a scene from mean girls. Almost comical. One day, we went out, and June was throwing a tantrum as any toddler would, I was worried as to how to fix this situation in public, she shoved me aside, looked at me in disgust, and picked June up. I couldn't believe my eyes. The insult got to the extent that I had gone to her village with her and her

mother had physically shoved me away from her daughter like I had some sort of disease.

Mr. Jay came later on that vacation and it soon occurred to me that he had been talking with them too as I lived in the house, intimating to them how horrible I was, carefully using them to torture me since he wasn't there to do it himself. To date, the friendship will never be the same as it was, and that's

only because I felt so betrayed beyond words. Mr jay later showed up and I understood what was going on. As soon as he landed, he ordered that I didn't perform the show I had been planning since the beginning of the festivities. Note that all year long, I was only allowed to be a housewife and even in December, I was not able to perform. In his words, if I performed the show I had been promoting all month long, we were going to be

divorced. Words cannot express how caged I felt. In the presence of everyone, I stood up for myself and performed my show. He eventually showed up at the show and pretended to be the most supporting spouse to the amazement of my family and friends who witnessed the hell he raised just a few hours prior. My father counseled us, put us in prayer and fasting, and even went on his knees to Mr. Jay to please not destroy his family name by

dissolving the marriage. We went back to America with high hopes.

One week back to US soil, Mr. Jay smashed June's room door to get in as I ran in there for refuge. We were having a conversation and I dared to say, we can agree to disagree. He smashed my phone again and this time, I held June so tight. We both cried ourselves to sleep. Mr. Jay was sick and no amount of fasting and praying or walking around on eggshells could fix it, I couldn't fix it.

CHAPTER 6
I AM LEAVING

The next day, I was done. I was committed to leaving this man. I was convinced that June couldn't watch this every other day and have a good life. It was up to me to save my baby. Growing up, I never got to see my parents fight. I told him I was leaving, and this time, he could see it in my eyes that I was done. He opened up and told me a story about his childhood. I am not going to share here as it is not mine to share. He claimed this was the reason he was hurting me. In my benevolence, I decided we could fix this again. If only I don't talk back, make sure I look him in the eyes as he screamed at me, and never aired my opinions.

I could fix it. You don't leave something that isn't working, you fix it! You don't throw away your broken toys, you fix them. This I taught my daughter. I resolved to stay.

Again.

I was made to get a therapist. Mr jay insisted that my goal in therapy was that we work on my 'control issues' and my 'rape victim' mentality, after I opened up to him about my trauma, he called me a rape victim for months and then topped it with the fact that I didn't make more than a Macdonald's employee. I was a classic rape victim, and all his psychologist friends agree. All his friends said so too. I believed him.

Therapy was mandatory for everyone who had had some sort of mental break. I started to talk to my therapist about the happenings at home. She insisted that before I went on medication, I had to get a psychological evaluation.

She recommended a Dr with some melanin in Beverly Hills.

I went in for the Evaluation. We had a lengthy conversation that involved detailing to him how I was convinced I was bipolar. He listened carefully and said nothing.

There was a fight again, he didn't come home all

day till 11 pm I stayed up, waiting for him, hoping to get his attention. Trying to get a glimpse of that love,

the beginning love, the love I was willing to defy the world for. That sweet, love- bombing love.

He came in the door, he was drunk, picked my daughter up, and said to her, 'do you know your mother is a whore, a bitch, a cunt'? Little June was beginning to comprehend things. We were at her 100th word, she knew when a word was bad, she said no daddy, he repeated, 'your mother is a whore, she is a cunt'. I couldn't handle it! I pushed him away and grabbed my daughter, that was the cue he was waiting for. He gave me a stinking slap on my face, so resounding my daughter screamed out. I didn't. I went cold and silent. As soon as he did this, he went straight to his phone to call his mother. His mother picked up the phone. 'I slapped her mom', and I chimed in, 'Mr. Jay slapped me in front of June', Mother returned, 'well it sounds like you both were going at it with each other'.

I was shocked. I was broken. For a moment I didn't think I could hear with that ear anymore. Under my breath, I whispered, 'I don't blame you mum, I knew you will protect your monster of a son'.

Mr Jay was married before.

At the beginning of the relationship, I wanted to reach out to her, just to speak to her but he strongly discouraged it saying she cheated on him and he caught her having intercourse with another man. I found that repulsive.

I decided to listen to my incumbent husband.

The love of my life at the time.

CHAPTER 7

TOXIC CYCLE

Mr. Jay was the nicest again, for the next few days after the slap. It was all smiles and happiness, as usual, a gift to make amends as usual. We were all rejoicing, it had been a full month without fighting or any abuse. My pee started to smell different! I am pregnant!

My fantasy of a happy family was finally materializing. I was grateful. Maybe it was going to be a cute baby boy, maybe Mr. Jay had changed. I was excited but true to the cycle. One afternoon after brunch, an argument ensued. At this point, I had begun to receive therapy and I was learning how to deescalate fights. One of the tactics I learned was to give ample space for each party to blaze and then calm down. As I attempted to go for a walk, he yanked me back, sending a shock wave from my shoulder straight to my waist. 'Where do you think you are going' he said. A few days later, I bled out. The baby came out in huge blood clots after hours of cramping.

I told his mum, and she said, 'Well you can't blame him for

that, it is not fair'.

I called my dad, 'I lost the baby daddy'. He went silent. The silence was bad.

Silence meant my dad had reached his limit.

I realized that the threats to leave weren't working anymore. They didn't stop him from doing what he needed. The day after the abuse was euphoric, and he seemed so happy. I was in love so I was happy when he was happy. I am an ex-commando, I grew up with abuse and I can take it. This is what I thought. If it mean I keep my family intact. The theory he taught me was that I was the reason he abused me. I was the cause of his anxiety and rage. He had never done this to anyone but me. And that if only I changed my stupid ways, he wouldn't have to abuse me.

I tried hard to change to fit into what he wanted, I was not allowed to eat gluten, go out, or have friends that were not related to work.

So I developed a system, the less time we spent together, the less time we had to argue in front of June, and the less time he had to notice my silly behaviors that made him so angry.

I found that I was getting some coins anytime I went live on Facebook. I so desperately wanted to be financially independent of this man so I decided to continue doing more lives and take it very seriously. I treated it like a 9-5. Creating and posting and going live. One reel, one live a day was my formula and it was working. He liked to see the money so I let him oversee it. He was an admin on my page and controlled everything. We would argue occasionally about my dance expressions and how he thought some were trashy and how everyone except me thought that I was a whore selling sex. I was just trying to create in

my truest essence. It didn't stop him from finding any and every opportunity to either call be a bitch or a whore.

I tried to break this toxic cycle by getting a nanny, if there was another

person in the house,
There probably will not be
any abuse, I pitched the
idea and it flew, I put out
a call and got one,

CHAPTER 8

MY NANNY EXPERIENCE

In one week, she seemed nice, I showed her around, where she could sleep, her pay was good everything seemed great. I urged him to work more using a new home as the goal while I doubled down on work as well to make sure to exhaust myself to complete

mush I didn't have the energy to engage when he tried to argue, so I didn't have the energy to bite the bait. The plan was working, things were looking great until I blurred the boundaries with the nanny. Being cooped up in the house together, we started to talk and I let her in on a little of my plight. It felt great to release to a stranger and we started to bond.

5 days post arrival, the nanny starts to complain about her phone and how she couldn't receive calls, I thought that a little strange as she was receiving calls just fine until she moved in. I had an iPhone I used to help me create content. It was amazing for playing the music while I did the dancing, She had her eye

on it and hinted that she wanted it.

I was not sure I was not ready to part with it just yet as she was getting paid in full and could buy hers with a month's worth of pay, this was a phone I used for work. She went ahead and told Mr Jay what she wanted it. I found that a little forward.

This nanny was a dancer, and occasionally I found her dancing for Mr Jay. I guess he was analyzing things I didn't know. I didn't want to be that paranoid wife checking to see if my nanny and husband were already having an affair. I had my insecurities but I didn't let them control me.

They started to get close, and the topic of closure

was me. I was caught in this triangulation I couldn't understand. She's crazy, she's bipolar, and I have to endure all this craziness living with her. It's not easy to be with her.

1 week after the in-home nanny moved in, Mr jay shows up from work and

tells me, he doesn't feel like seeing my face that

night, and that I needed to find a place to sleep. I was shocked. He ordered me to get out of the house at 9 pm, leaving June, this new nanny, and his home alone. I in utter shock, I got into my car and started to make calls to find where I could sleep, you see, I was surrounded by followers but I had no true friends, this is because, once I got remotely close to anyone, Mr. Jay cornered them and

told them lies about how I was bipolar and crazy and how he was barely surviving being with me. Unconsciously I cut off all my friends because I couldn't afford this getting to the blogs who already enjoyed vilifying me for my lifestyle choices. I checked the account we shared which was my only account in America. It had $0.00 in there. I was petrified. This man had emptied my account and ordered me out of his house in the middle of the night in LA and I had no one to call. I was lost. Words are not enough to describe how I felt on that day. I was vibrating in the car as I scrolled through all my contacts and realized how isolated I was. F?*k! How did I get here? The tears couldn't stop pouring.

I had not maintained a relationship with anyone I could call after being kicked out of my home. It was pathetic. I was pathetic, I

hated myself for letting me get to this. I was sick

in my stomach. I scrolled and scrolled and landed on my dear friend Maya, one of the only women I had invited to our small wedding in Lekki, Maya was a mover and shaker. ' Maya, I need your help, Mr Jay just kicked me out of our home with no money in the joint account'. As I speak I do not have a dollar to my name, I need to poop and

I can't even go in my house where my daughter is!'

Be Calm Korra, go to this address, there is a key under the mat, go there, use the bathroom, and sleep. Maya saved me that night and for that, I'll always be grateful. I was headed to Venice, and that night I cried myself to sleep as I made sure I drank all the liquor I could find to numb the pain I was feeling inside. In the morning, I went over to the house. The nanny was charging her new iPhone, my work phone,

while June sat there eating her breakfast, I walked in and she asked ' Did Mr jay say you could come back here?'

I couldn't breathe, and she proceeded to call

him, pacing back and forth like I was tresspassing on her private property. I showed this woman where she could sleep in my home and now this. I got in the bedroom, Got naked, and started to cry, I cried to GOD! Oh God, please see

me through. I am penniless in America, all my money emptied by this man, and my daughter didn't even interact with me. I was replaced one week after this new nanny arrived. I couldn't hold back my tears. Reality hit me like a boulder that night. I was not married, I was alone and co-living with my worst enemy. That night was a turning point for my heart. I told my family about this incident and the elders already started severing

spiritual ties with Mr. Jay, we were done.

I took a shower, looked at myself in the mirror, and decided, this is not my life. This is not my story. Mr. Jay and the new nanny had ganged up together. It was an uncomfortable couple of days as I refused to leave my own home again, eventually, the nanny left, but not without threatening to call child services for alleged negligence, it became apparent to me

that Mr Jay pitched me as a horrible mother to any ear willing to listen, he had perfected this speech it was so believable. Hence the nanny, and my friend's reaction to me, even after they saw they saw the way I treated my daughter firsthand. If my husband is complaining then it must be true. He ended up paying her $2000. In my mind, I knew no one gives someone something that big if they have nothing on them. She left but not

without raining curses on me on her way out, which

included, me being a whore, negligent mother, etc. as I can't remember all. Till today Mr. Jay's ability to manipulate is still a shock to me sometimes. I wonder how he was able to control this woman so easily, a woman I had trusted with my story had done a 180 degree turnaround and became his ally in less than a day.

I was working. Determined to gain financial independence. KORRA IS LIVE was born, I was live for anything and everything. I got closer to my fans than ever. I was hungry. I started to go live when he was home to reduce the amount of time I had to speak to him. The less we spoke, the less likely it was for him to smash my phone, call me a cunt/bitch or belittle me to the full glare of my daughter.

Things were good again and my dream of a happy family was still alive, although I knew this was a toxic situation, I was convinced I was tough enough to handle it but not dumb enough to think I was protected, I don wise up. God does not give his worse fights to weak ones I thought. I was determined to work through marriage for my daughter. I wanted her to see that a family was possible. However, if I was to do this I had to come

down from cloud nine and use my brain. We got pregnant again. I was determined for my girl to be free. I didn't know what my motivation was but somehow I felt a sense of urgency. I felt like there was an impending emergency I had to get ready for. I was working. I thought documenting my pregnancy journey would be amazing and help with the money, I pitched the idea, and he resisted but finally agrees, with restrictions and roadblocks here and there that I had to carefully navigate through to have the dream of documenting this come through.

CHAPTER 10
SHOW ME THE MONEY

God blessed me and the monies started to pour in. I opened up my account and deposited my monies in there as per my father's instructions. This didn't seat well with Mr. Jay who forced me to send my paycheck to him every month. He said the government needed him to pay his student loans Asap and the urgent stories about the interest rates. One day I was screamed at from 9am - 4pm and he didn't stop until I transferred $10,000 to him.

I was 4 months pregnant.

He had removed me as his admin on Instagram and changed his password right after I grew his page to over 100,000 followers. I found this a little odd. I decided that since I wasn't an admin on his page, he couldn't be one on my page as well. I tried to remove him over and over and he refused vehemently stating that he had to be an admin and anything I had was his and vice versa. I pointed out that I had no idea what he had because I had no access to any accounts, or passwords, nothing. He didn't budge. As soon as

I got monetized, I had to send a total contribution of $40,000 towards his student loans. That was all I had to my name at the time. I was back to square one. No money in my bank account. It still didn't make him happy, this 'whore' who didn't make more than a 'Macdonald's employee' according to him, just contributed immensely to clearing off some debt and he was still upset that I had

not given him more, sighting the urgency of the payments and how he had a deadline to fulfill. We had been married for 4 years. I was so confused because these loans had been present since I had known him.Why the sudden urgency? I started to suspect foul play.

He went to work daily as early as 6am and came back at midnight including on weekends. He publicly claimed to have $2000 days, which made $14000 weeks so why did he need my money so bad?

I was tired. I felt so used and abused, heavily pregnant, and still having to do everything by myself even down to washing my car at 9 months pregnant all for my husband to swoop in to collect all I had made month after month. This was modern-day slavery as I didn't have any other words to describe my situation. The days I didn't remit my paycheck, he made my life a living hell, screaming down at me for what will be hours, all while demanding sex whenever he wanted.

At 4.5 months pregnant, he decided on a work trip to the Dominican Republic, he then asked that I and June come to visit him there, I love to travel. I was so happy and grateful. I packed our bags and we headed over. On arrival

there, post travel sex, my privates swole up like a ripe plum, apparently, he had been a dog and given me something. While pregnant with Athena, he placed me on a course of antibiotics, this was very dangerous for Athena, and he blamed what I caught on the hotel pool. What was strange is he took the antibiotics too.

I didn't want to believe anything else as I was too fragile physically and emotionally to comprehend

anything in that vulnerable state so I decided to play dumb.

The big day was finally drawing close, the birth of

the goddess of war and wisdom. Black mold was discovered at our current residence so we had to move, to move, we had to sign a lease. This lease was completely 60/40 with me paying a huge part of the rent and one extra month, making a total of $13,000 I sent to my then-husband to

pay for the move. As usual online, he made it

seem like he did it and moved us after working so hard while I was pregnant. In retrospect, I am happy I did. I will not victimize myself because I wanted to bring honor to my husband, I love deeply and that is what I do when I love. I made him look so good even when I was still being abused while heavily pregnant. As soon as we moved in, there were 2 rooms, he converted one to his office and spent hours

there, locked up. It was to be a home birth so we had to prepare, Athena was taking longer than expected to come out and it was a high-stress environment, it was barely 1 week into living in the new house that he began to scream at me for hours again, I forget what happened but I remember me walking to the roof deck just to breathe and he began to charge at me like he was running to come hit me, I was 9 months + pregnant and

heavy with Athena walking away to deescalate and he charged me like a bull. I knew that Athena whose birth was supposed to glue us together only drove us farther apart, we weren't working and we knew it.

It was time to pay for Athena's birth, but he simply refused, 'You are making money, why can't you pay for her birth'? He belted at me. For there to be peace, I paid for my daughter's birth. When I had to explain to my therapist that my Dr husband, who is making 6 figures, monies that I never saw, was not interested in paying for the birth of our daughter, I couldn't hold back my tears.

If you do not take anything from this book, take the beauty of therapy, pouring everything out to a stranger is such a gift. I am so grateful for the perspective therapy gave

me. I was able to zoom out and look at my life from an outsider's perspective. I was able to notice what I was too close to see in the past. Therapy was and still is one of the factors that saved my life.

THE STRENGTH OF ATHENA

After 2 weeks of waiting, I drank 8 ounces of castor oil and Athena arrived 3 hours later.

Athena was born! The miracle I had been waiting for was here!

While pushing, Mr. Jay and June caught Athena.

Something extreme shifted in me after

Athena's birth. I wasn't scared anymore. I felt so strong. Giving birth in my bedroom was one of the most liberating experiences of my life. I think Mr. Jay could

sense it. Little Bambi was not so little anymore.

I knew after Athena, I couldn't continue suffering and smiling. That was when the worse happened. Till today, I don't know what came over Mr jay, it was like he was on drugs or something. Athena came out 'face first' and when she came out, she had sores all over her face, I turned around to ask Jay, what is up with her face. I was told that it will all clear up in no time by my Midwife. Mr jay became a psychiatrist overnight, diagnosing me of dissociation disorder. He accused me of wanting to kill my own child. It was just three hours after delivery.

 I just couldn't understand what was going on. I was so confused. He was pacing back and forth like a deranged man. I didn't know what to make of it.

He started to threaten me as usual, 'I'm going to take the kids from you' he said. We had barely even celebrated the birth of the new baby, what is going on, I was worried. Maybe something shifted in him too, having to catch Athena.

I was worried for him, what if he wasn't okay. He started to threaten to take June and Athena, again. Who does this to a mother who just gave birth hours ago?

Is he joking? Is this April fools?

He gets his backup on the phone as usual, his mother, he continues, 'I am taking the kids, you are a horrible mother, how can you ask me what is wrong with Athena's face? In psychology that is a sign, you will kill your kids, you are a horrible mother'.

I was still bleeding heavily. I had no idea why this man who was supposed to be helping me was doing this to me.

I started to employ all the tactics I learned in therapy, I couldn't go for a walk as I was bleeding, Athena was still red! The midwife and assistants had just left. I tried everything, I started to beg. It only escalated more as June watched. Same cycle!

On Athena's birthday!

I cried myself to sleep as I was bombarded with congratulations on IG. Even my fake happy place couldn't bring me out of this depression. Regret was all I felt, regret making this man my head, my King, this man was nobody's King but lived only for himself.

I wish my daughters didn't have to go through this. I regret choosing you. I had never voiced this out before. It was so liberating. I was

heartbroken and for the first time, I was admitting it to myself instead of creating fake universes to hide in, I had made a mistake with a partner and I was finally accepting it. He came in as I struggled to get Athena to latch. He started to taunt me like he did when I lost my mind, repeat what you said! Repeat it. I looked up, what are you doing? Repeat it! He was LIVE this time! He was going to destroy my Korraverse. My safe space, he was going to take my

kids, and my fans and leave me hanging dry again to his full delight.

Oh my God! He posted! I am divorcing Korra, I left Athena, and went straight to my knees. To the floor. Please I beg you. Please don't do this, my sister begged, my father, begged, and my elders prayed. We don't have a lot, but we have a good name, the Obidi family is not associated with divorce. No problem cannot be fixed.

The entire village was activated.

We all begged. I held on to his feet as he kicked me away like a leper.

He had gone too far. Delete it! Please! We have 2 daughters. Please look at your newborn. She is still fresh out of the womb. Please consider us. I groveled for hours as my infant cried for her mother. He refused! I have to protect myself, he retorted. I didn't understand what he

meant but when all the news articles in the country started to pour in, there was no protecting anything.

He came from work one morning, while I was in bed with Athena, he started to try to start an argument, I was not interested, he grabbed my phone from me and started to delete things. Voicenotes and all evidences of abuse he could find. Give me back my phone I yelled as Athena was in my arms. He didn't

listen and went straight for the door, I placed Athena down and started to chase after him, give me my phone! Give it to me! My family soon started to realize who they were dealing with.

The truth started to pour like a flood. He had an affair with a 19-year-old who was threatening him, he threw me under the towel just to save skin. She had seen he welcomed a second child after claiming to have had a vasectomy, she had unprotected sex with him for weeks in Brazil, and she couldn't stand it. Why he couldn't tell me so we could figure or work it out is what I don't understand. I guess he was sick of him too and decided to end it before she went public.

Then came the lies about me. I watched how people who have hated me for years started to spew lies about me, she's going down, let's sink that ship. It

was the lesson of a lifetime. I watched it, and I read everything. My heart broke as Athena drank every last drop of my disappointment in her breast milk. My breasts dried up like a well in the desert when I saw a video of my husband defaming me, saying I slept with men, and participated in orgies, as the media houses flew with it, happy to burn the internet whore at a stake.

He told me to leave the house, move out! I was not surprised, I knew he wanted his cream home to himself, my use was over. It was raining so I took the girls out in the car and started to search for apartments. Athena was only days old. He came and lied that a Dr wanted to examine Athena, He said he was happy to watch them as I looked for a place to live. I thanked him and I handed the kids over to him, I searched all day and found a place. After

what seemed like a successful house search

day, I came back to the apartment, it was empty!

Where are my kids? ' "I took the kids Korra," Mr. Jay said.

All the years of threats were now a reality. I lost consciousness and fell straight to the ground.

My knees buckled under the weight of my body.

You did what? I started to hyperventilate. Where is my infant?

Please I beg you. She is a week old. I will do anything, please. I called his mom, 'Mum, Mr Jay has taken my new born away, can you please talk to him?' To my utter amazement, she returned, 'well, you know, divorces are messy.'

I slumped straight to the floor like a sack of potatoes.

I almost died. Please I beg you. Do not separate me from my infant. This is not normal, are you trying to kill me? She went off the phone. I called every mutual friend I could, I was shaking and I couldn't breathe. I called him, I was able to get him on the phone. The sickest thing that still boggles my mind is, he insisted on a video call, just to watch me wailing. Mr Jay please where is Athena, where are you. 'Im afraid, I can't tell you that, as he watched intently as I cried

with veins all over my face' as he enjoyed it.

Truth is, this entire this was a classic case of greed. Till date I have never seen a human react to money the way he did, it was fascinating. He was going to end me if it meant he could to get his hands on the money that I dared to put in my own account. He ripped my kids from me, hopefully to get me back in the hospital, withdraw all the money, and abscond with the kids.

I was slipping into a depression and my milk was drying up. For 2 days I didn't know where my kids were. I was pleading. I kept on begging, but it was like I was speaking to a rock. He was feeding Athena unmixed formula on his friend's couch on his Live video, I watch it crying uncontrollably. My tits were engorged and heavy with her milk yet he was giving

her formula just to torture me. Not caring about the baby. This was hard to experience in private, let alone to the full glare of the public.

Once news of our divorce hit the media, the worst happened. Several women started to reach out about their experience with Mr. Jay. You see, let me take your mind back to earlier when I mentioned that as soon as he had hit 100,000 followers on instagram, his

account, which I managed for the longest time was removed from my manage list, he changed his password and immediately took me off everything. It turns out that the reason he did this was to cyber-molest women in the guise of helping them with back pain. A few reached out saying they had asked for a consultation with him, he offered them a free consult if he could use the information as part of his studies. He then directed them to WhatsApp and told them in order to help, he had to see their breasts, Many women said they didn't even know what they were doing until it was all over. He had manipulated many women into showing their bodies to him.

This was the final straw.

'LA mom', swept in like an angel. She was in my ear. Reminding me, You've got this. You can do this, she woke me up with prayers, and she nudged

me towards my Creator. She recruited her entire village. Aunty Ozor, Aunty Aduke, My entire family showed up from nowhere. My own Nkem, Nancy rose to my defense, she fought for me, Stevana stood like a warrior, he was going to come to pick up some breast milk and she served him the restraining order that brought my kids back in my arms. Dolapo came through for me, helping with looking for apartments, it was divine, these women made sure I didn't go under. My lovers, my fans.

They saved my mind from reclining at those crucial times.

I watched long-time friends take sides with the Oyinbo who they assumed was the secret of my success, the 'white is right mentality' was and is still very real. It was sickening to see him going on with his smear campaign, amassing thousands of followers of people who hated my guts.

I had two options, get my milk flowing back for my daughters or seat and let my myself slip into postpartum depression. I picked option one. I picked myself up and got to MOVING.

WE MOVE.

He wanted me to pay his rent for a year. I knew I had to lawyer up. I rented a U-Haul. I started to move my things.

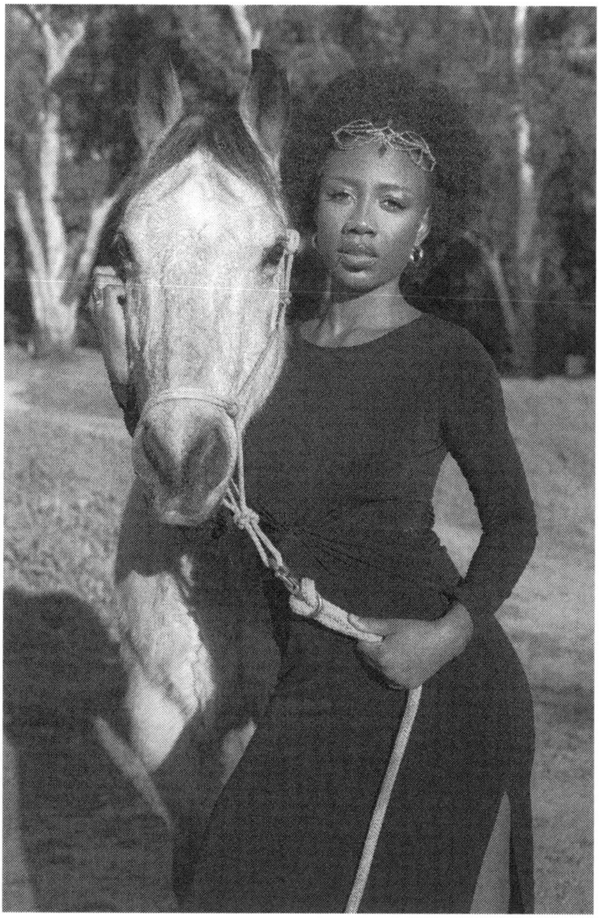

FREEDOM

My first day in my small apartment, I was so emotional, I was flooded with grief and fear. I imagined leaving to be the death of me, but this time, I made it. Thanks to my Angels on Earth. Right after the fear came bliss. I consulted with my

Therapist and that night was the beginning of the rest of my life, the journey so far is a testimony. I am in a one bedroom apartment but it feels like heaven to wake up

and not be abused. Verbally or physically.

Guess I celebrated too soon as Mr. Jay started to file ExPartes to separate my daughters from me again. It has been a combination of hell and bliss fighting for my daughters these past months as you all know. Now that I think about it, I was to be used as a free surrogate and once, Athena was out, My use expired. However, E shock am. I will fight to my last breath. June and Athena, my love for you is like the ocean. Endless!

I have threatened serially with my life, I might return in a sequel if everything goes well.

I will love you till the end of time. I will fight for a million years. Yours truly. Your singing dancing princess from the Motherland.

Printed in Great Britain
by Amazon